For my sister, Dr. Sharon Churnin Nash, a mover of mountains, who has been indefatigable in her loving support as I move mine.

I would like to thank my wonderful editor and publisher, Marissa Moss, and my agent, Karen Grencik of Red Fox Literary, who move mountains every day to bring stories to children that inspire, delight, and remind us that everyone, everywhere has the power to make a difference for good in the world. My thanks also to Rachel Ball-Phillips, lecturer at Southern Methodist University, her daughter, Leora Phillips, Sarah Hanan of SMU, my husband, Michael Granberry, and my boys, Ted, Sam. David, and Josh. And thank you to children everywhere for opening these pages, letting Manjhi into your hearts, and, I hope, being inspired to be kind. For each kindness chips away at the mountains that separate us and can make a mighty difference in the world. May you move mountains. Always.
— N.C.

For Ollie, my four-legged mountain buddy.
— D.P.

Book design by Simon Stahl

CIP data for this book is available from the Library of Congress.

Published by Creston Books, LLC
www.crestonbooks.co

Type set in Bookman and Caslon

Manufactured in Dongguan, China by R.R. Donnelley
5

Manjhi Moves a Mountain

By
Nancy Churnin

Illustrated by
Danny Popovici

Creston Books

Deep in the heart of India, a mighty mountain separated two villages.

On Manjhi's side, nothing grew. People were hungry. Children gave up walking the 40 long miles to school on the other side of the mountain. Adults groaned on the jagged long climb to plough the fields or shop at the market.

On the other side, rice and wheat flowered and flourished. People's bellies were full and their pockets jangled with money.

Every day, Manjhi paused at the top of the mountain to catch his breath and gaze at the two villages. Why should some people have so much and others so little?

Manjhi tried to think of an answer as he made his way down the mountain to plant and harvest on the other side.

If only the two villages were closer. If only the road between them were easier. If only there were a way to move the mountain!

Frustrated, he picked up a stone and threw it down.

Crack!

He saw a sprinkle of powder. He knelt down and felt it between his fingers.

That was it!

Manjhi hurried to his hut to search for something to trade. He had nothing anyone would want except three goats. He gently looped ropes around their necks and searched until he found someone who would trade a worn hammer and chisel for them.

He hurried back to the top of the mountain. He positioned the chisel. He aimed. He swung the hammer.

Clink!

Powdered rock and tiny chips sprayed.

Over and over, Manjhi swung, until it was too dark to see.

Clink! Clank! Clunk!

His sweaty, throbbing fingers rubbed the rough rock. He felt a dent. It was small and bumpy, but it was there.

Two inches, three inches.

His shoulders ached, his head pounded. But his heart was lighter. He picked his way down the mountain and across the dirt path. He tumbled into bed.

All too soon, a rooster crowed. Manjhi rubbed his eyes. His hands were raw with blisters. Still he climbed the mountain. He gripped the hammer and pounded the chisel for hours.

Hold. Aim. Swing!

Then he scrambled down to hoe, water, and weed on the other side. As soon as he could, he rushed back up.

Hold. Aim. Swing!

Day after day, Manjhi clutched the hammer and chisel.
Hold. Aim. Swing!
Night after night, he slid dusty fingers into the hole, measuring.
One foot, two feet.
After a week, he could crouch inside.
Four feet, five feet.

You're crazy, people told him. A man can't change a mountain. It's there before he's born and after he dies.

But Manjhi could see something they couldn't: the parting of the mountain into two great halves with a road in between. A road where people could get to work, to market, to school, even to the hospital more easily. Nothing could stop him. Not words. Not time. Not even the mountain, which sent chips and powder tumbling down his shoulders, whitening his hair.

A year passed. Every day Manjhi was a little stronger and the hole a little deeper and longer.

Ten feet forward. Twenty feet forward.

Ten years passed. Still it was too far for children to walk to school, the sick often couldn't get to the clinic in time, and the villagers spent countless hours climbing to work in the fields and shop in the markets. But Manjhi didn't slow down.

Hold. Aim. Swing!

He pushed forward.

Thirty feet forward. Fifty feet forward.

The sides of the hole towered over his body!

After 15 years, people started to see what he had seen. Adults who had been children when he began, marveled. Children, who had never known a time when he wasn't striking the mountain, watched in awe.

One hundred feet forward. Two hundred feet forward.

Now each time he returned to his task, Manjhi could see that helping hands had made the hole a little longer than he'd left it. He found food waiting for him, too.

Baskets of warm roti dripping with melted ghee. Tins of spicy dahl tickled his nose. Once he unwrapped a cloth to find a shiny new hammer and chisel glinting in the sun.

By the 22nd year, whispers swept through both villages. Every day more people gathered. Parents lifted little ones on their shoulders so they could see the other side. They wondered if this would be the day.

Hold. Aim. Swing!

Men, women, children held their breath. Manjhi could hear his heart beating as loudly as the hammer hitting the rock.

Hold. Aim. Swing!

Swoosh!

Where once a mighty mountain stood, there was nothing but open space and broken rocks.

Manjhi looked from one village to the other, but for the first time, there weren't two villages.

There was just one, sharing water, hopes, dreams...and a man who had moved a mountain!

Author's Note

Dashrath Manjhi was born in 1934 and died Aug. 17, 2007 at the age of 73. Using only a chisel and a hammer, he took 22 years, from 1960-1982, to cut a road 360 feet long, 30 feet high and 25 feet wide through a mountain that blocked Gehlaur, his village near Gaya in Bihar, India, from Wazirganj, which had running water, doctors, a school, and jobs. For most of those years, Manjhi was ridiculed for pursuing an impossible goal. Not only was he a poor laborer, he was a Shudra, from one of the lowest castes in Hindu society. Those who follow the caste system believe people must live in certain places and have different access to jobs, schools, hospitals, and land according to the group in which they're born.

Manjhi began his task for his wife, Falguni Devi, who died in 1959, supporting his dream. For some, the story of Manjhi's parting of the mountain is a love story, done in dedication to his wife who had difficulty getting medical care. It's been compared to how the great emperor Shah Jahan of India built the Taj Mahal as a tomb for his wife, Mumtaz Mahal, from 1632-1643. Another image that comes to mind is that of the Hindu god Krishna who is said to have lifted Mount Govardhana to shelter a group of villagers from the rain.

What began as a labor for Manjhi's wife evolved into a determination to help his entire village, one of about 60 in the rocky, remote area. By shortening a treacherous 34-mile trek to a manageable 9-mile walk across a safe road, he changed everyone's lives for the better and gave them hope that there was nothing that couldn't be done if you believed and persevered.

When the Indian government gave Manjhi land as a reward for his impressive achievement, he donated it to his village for a hospital to be built there. The road he had carved made it easeir for teachers to come to his village, creating a new school. Not only did the road make it easier for the villagers to reach the world, it made it easier for the world to come to them.

Manjhi is honored in his village and all across India as the Mountain Man.

Move Your Own Mountain

Dashrath Manjhi wanted to make life better for everyone in his village. He didn't have money, but he had an idea – to make a path through the mountain – and was willing to work hard to make his dream come true. What kind of "mountain" can you move to make things better in your community? Some children have designated a "buddy bench" on their school playground so that a child without a friend can sit on the bench and someone will invite the child to play. Others have become buddies for kids with special needs, "adopted" seniors at retirement homes, or volunteered to walk or play with animals at shelters. Some children have started recycling programs. One California teen, Natalie Hampton, created a free Sit With Us app that helps kids find someone to sit with at lunch.

For more activities and ideas, go to crestonbooks.co and download a free curriculum guide. To share your ideas and see what others are doing, please go to nancychurnin.com where we're celebrating the many wonderful ways kids can move mountains!

NANCY CHURNIN is the author of *The William Hoy Story: How a Deaf Baseball Player Changed the Game*. She writes most days as the theater critic for *The Dallas Morning News* and grew up in New York City going to Broadway shows and Yankee games. She graduated from Harvard University cum laude and has a masters in journalism from Columbia University. She is raising four boys and two cats with her husband, *Dallas Morning News* arts writer Michael Granberry.

DANNY POPOVICI'S illustrations have appeared in many formats: animation, game, and comic art, but his favorite medium to tell stories is in the pages of magical picture books. He lives in Portland, Oregon, where there's no shortage of mountains to hike, but he usually leaves his hammer and chisel at home. *Manjhi Moves a Mountain* is Danny's debut. You can learn more about Danny at dannypopovici.com.